Award-Winn
of the
Country Music Association

ISBN 0-7935-8483-3

HAL•LEONARD®
CORPORATION

7777 W. BLUEMOUND RD. P.O. BOX 13819 MILWAUKEE, WI 53213

Visit Hal Leonard Online at
www.halleonard.com

Award-Winning Songs
of the
Country Music Association

Nominees and Winners of the CMA Song of the Year

5   **CMA Award-Winning Songwriters**
10   **Nominated Song of the Year Writers and Performers**
12   **CMA Awards Photos**

Song	*Recorded by*
18 Achy Breaky Heart	*Billy Ray Cyrus*
24 After All This Time	*Rodney Crowell*
28 Ain't That Lonely Yet	*Dwight Yoakam*
32 All My Ex's Live in Texas	*George Strait*
36 Baby's Got Her Blue Jeans On	*Mel McDaniel*
40 Boot Scootin' Boogie	*Brooks & Dunn*
44 Can't Stop My Heart from Lovin' You	*The O'Kanes*
54 Chattahoochee* *(1994)*	*Alan Jackson*
49 Check Yes or No	*George Strait*
58 Chiseled in Stone* *(1989)*	*Vern Gosdin*
62 Daddy's Hands	*Holly Dunn*
74 The Dance	*Garth Brooks*
78 Do Ya'	*K.T. Oslin*
84 Don't Close Your Eyes	*Keith Whitley*
88 Don't Rock the Jukebox	*Alan Jackson*
67 Down at the Twist and Shout	*Mary Chapin Carpenter*
92 Eighteen Wheels and a Dozen Roses	*Kathy Mattea*
97 80's Ladies* *(1988)*	*K.T. Oslin*
104 Forever and Ever, Amen* *(1987)*	*Randy Travis*
116 Friends in Low Places	*Garth Brooks*
127 Go Rest High on That Mountain* *(1996)*	*Vince Gill*

	Song	**Recorded by**
111	God Bless the U.S.A.* *(1985)*	*Lee Greenwood*
122	Gone Country	*Alan Jackson*
130	Grandpa (Tell Me 'Bout the Good Old Days)	*The Judds*
(134)	He Thinks He'll Keep Her	*Mary Chapin Carpenter*
144	Here's a Quarter (Call Someone Who Cares)	*Travis Tritt*
150	I Still Believe in You* *(1993)*	*Vince Gill*
139	I Swear	*John Michael Montgomery*
154	If Tomorrow Never Comes	*Garth Brooks*
159	Independence Day* *(1995)*	*Martina McBride*
164	The Keeper of the Stars	*Tracy Byrd*
(169)	A Little Good News	*Anne Murray*
(172)	Little Rock	*Collin Raye*
178	Look at Us* *(1992)*	*Vince Gill*
183	Lost in the Fifties Tonight (In the Still of the Nite)	*Ronnie Milsap*
186	Love, Me	*Collin Raye*
191	On the Other Hand* *(1986)*	*Randy Travis*
194	Thinkin' Problem	*David Ball*
200	Time Marches On	*Tracy Lawrence*
205	When I Call Your Name* *(1991)*	*Vince Gill*
208	Where've You Been* *(1990)*	*Kathy Mattea*
212	The Wind Beneath My Wings* *(1984)*	*Gary Morris*

*CMA Song of the Year

Through the Country Music Association's leadership and guidance, Country Music has become one of America's most diplomatic ambassadors to the world. Industry leaders readily admit that CMA has won global recognition and has been the most important force in the worldwide growth and expansion of Country Music. The first trade organization ever formed to promote a type of music, CMA, founded in 1958, originally consisted of only 233 members and now boasts more than 7,000 members in 40 countries.

One of CMA's most significant achievements is the CMA Awards which has been on national television each year since 1968. Considered the Country Music industry's most highly-coveted and pre-eminent awards, the accolades are presented annually to outstanding Country artists and songwriters, as voted by CMA's membership, to honor excellence in artistry. Membership in CMA is open to those persons or organizations presently or formerly active, directly or indirectly, in the field of Country Music.

Any Country Music song with original words and music is eligible for the CMA Song of the Year nomination, based upon the song's Country singles chart activity during the eligibility period, which spans from July 1 through June 30 of each year. Nominations from the CMA membership, in addition to the top five songs from the combined tabulation of the Country singles charts from BILLBOARD, THE GAVIN REPORT, and RADIO & RECORDS, are voted on through balloting by the entire CMA membership. From this, the top five songs appear on the final ballot with Song of the Year being selected and first announced on the CMA Awards telecast.

CMA AWARD-WINNING SONGWRITERS

Photo Courtesy of CMA/
Don Putnam, Photographer

JEFF SILBAR and LARRY HENLEY
1984 – "Wind Beneath My Wings"

Photo Courtesy of CMA/
Don Putnam, Photographer

LEE GREENWOOD
1985 — "God Bless The U.S.A."

Photo Courtesy of CMA/
Beth Gwinn, Photographer

DON SCHLITZ, RANDY TRAVIS (Performer) and PAUL OVERSTREET
1986 — "On The Other Hand"

Photo Courtesy of CMA/
Alan Mayor, Photographer

DON SCHLITZ, PAUL OVERSTREET and RANDY TRAVIS (Performer)
1987 — "Forever And Ever, Amen"

Photo Courtesy of CMA/
Beth Gwinn, Photographer

K.T. OSLIN
1988 — "80's Ladies"

Photo Courtesy of CMA/
Beth Gwinn, Photographer

MAX D. BARNES (with VERN GOSDIN)
1989 — "Chiseled In Stone"

Photo Courtesy of CMA/
Beth Gwinn, Photographer

JON VEZNER and DON HENRY
1990 — "Where've You Been"

Photo Courtesy of CMA/
Alan L. Mayor, Photographer

VINCE GILL AND TIM DUBOIS
1991 — "When I Call Your Name"

Photo Courtesy of CMA/
Alan L. Mayor, Photographer

VINCE GILL
1992 — "Look At Us"

Photo Courtesy of CMA/
Alan L. Mayor, Photographer

ALAN JACKSON
1994 — "Chattahoochee"

Photo Courtesy of CMA/
Chris Hollo, Photographer

GRETCHEN PETERS
1995 — "Independence Day"

NOMINATED SONG OF THE YEAR
WRITERS AND/OR PERFORMERS

Photo Courtesy of CMA/
Alan Mayor, Photographer

GEORGE STRAIT

Photo Courtesy of CMA/
Beth Gwinn, Photographer

RANDY TRAVIS

Photo Courtesy of CMA/
Beth Gwinn, Photographer

NAOMI and WYNONNA/THE JUDDS

Photo Courtesy of CMA/
Alan Mayor, Photographer

DAN SEALS

Photo Courtesy of CMA/
Alan Mayor, Photographer

HOLLY DUNN

Photo Courtesy of CMA
Beth Gwinn, Photographer

JAMIE O'HARA and KIERAN KANE/THE O'KANES

CMA AWARDS
SHOW PHOTOS

DAVE LOGGINS and ANNE MURRAY

Photo Courtesy of CMA/
Beth Gwinn, Photographer

RONNIE MILSAP and KENNY ROGERS

Photo Courtesy of CMA/
Alan Mayor, Photographer

WILLIE NELSON and KRIS KRISTOFFERSON

Photo Courtesy of CMA/
Alan Mayor, Photographer

LORETTA LYNN and CONWAY TWITTY

Photo Courtesy of CMA
Don Putnam, Photographer

WILLIE NELSON, KRIS KRISTOFFERSON, WAYLON JENNINGS and JOHNNY CASH

Photo Courtesy of CMA/
Beth Gwinn, Photographer

TANYA TUCKER

Photo Courtesy of CMA/
Beth Gwinn, Photographer

DWIGHT YOAKAM and BUCK OWENS

*Photo Courtesy of CMA/
Beth Gwinn, Photographer*

KATHY MATTEA

*Photo Courtesy of CMA/
Beth Gwinn, Photographer*

HANK WILLIAMS , JR.

Photo Courtesy of CMA/
Beth Gwinn, Photographer

REBA McENTIRE

Photo Courtesy of CMA/
Beth Gwinn, Photographer

GARTH BROOKS

Photo Courtesy of CMA/
Beth Gwinn, Photographer

DON HENRY, KATHY MATTEA, and JON VEZNER

Photo Courtesy of CMA/
Alan L. Mayor, Photographer

PAM TILLIS

Photo Courtesy of CMA/
Alan L. Mayor, Photographer

VINCE GILL and PATTY LOVELESS

Photo Courtesy of CMA/
Alan L. Mayor, Photographer

CLINT BLACK and ROY ROGERS

ACHY BREAKY HEART
(Don't Tell My Heart)

Words and Music by
DON VON TRESS

might blow__ up and kill this man. Ooh._____

man.

AFTER ALL THIS TIME

Words and Music by
RODNEY CROWELL

AIN'T THAT LONELY YET

Words and Music by KOSTAS
and JAMES HOUSE

ALL MY EX'S LIVE IN TEXAS

Words and Music by SANGER D. SHAFER
and LINDA J. SHAFER

All my ex - 's live in

Tex - as,   and Tex - as is a place___ I'd dear - ly

35

BABY'S GOT HER BLUE JEANS ON

Words and Music by
BOB McDILL

Moderately Fast

Down on the cor - ner by the traf - fic light ev' - ry - bod - y's look - in'

as she goes by.___ They turn their heads___ and they watch her till___ she's gone.

Lord, have mer - cy! Ba - by's got her blue jeans on.___

BOOT SCOOTIN' BOOGIE

Words and Music by
RONNIE DUNN

CAN'T STOP MY HEART FROM LOVIN' YOU

Words and Music by JAMIE O'HARA
and KIERAN KANE

CHECK YES OR NO

Words and Music by DANNY M. WELLS
and DANA H. OGLESBY

CHATTAHOOCHEE

Words and Music by JIM McBRIDE
and ALAN JACKSON

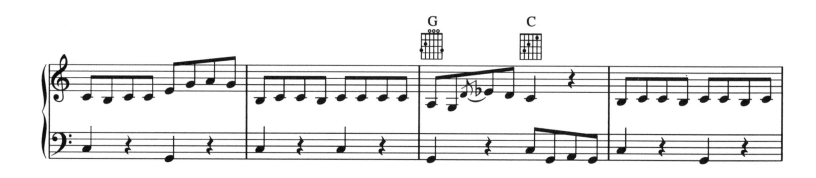

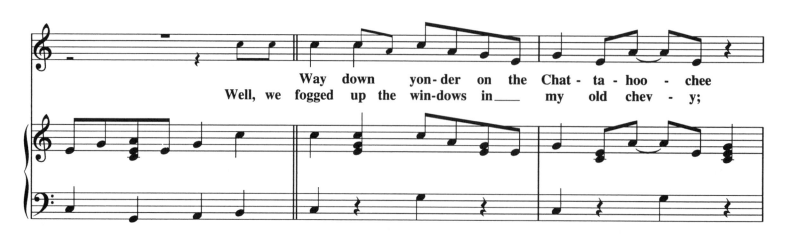

Way down yon-der on the Chat-ta-hoo-chee
Well, we fogged up the win-dows in___ my old chev-y;

CHISELED IN STONE

Words and Music by VERN GOSDIN
and MAX D. BARNES

See addtional lyrics

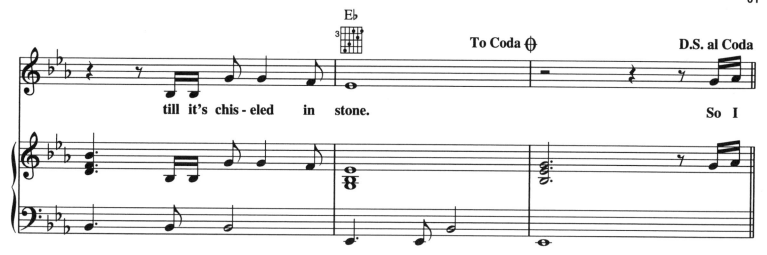

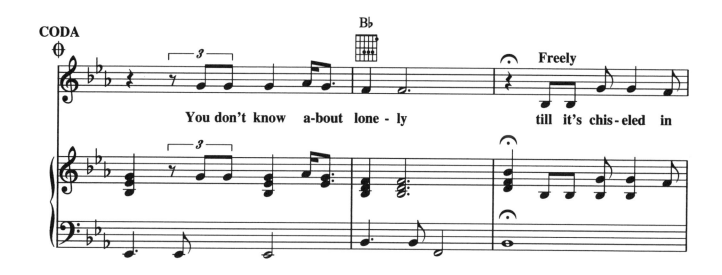

Additional Lyrics

2. Then an old man sat beside me
   And looked me in the eye.
   He said, "Son, I know what you're goin' through.
   But you oughta get down on your knees
   And thank your lucky stars
   That you've got someone to go home to."
   Chorus

3. So I brought these pretty flowers
   Hopin' you would understand
   Sometimes a man is such a fool.
   These golden words of wisdom
   From the heart of that old man
   Showed me I ain't nothin' without you.
   Chorus

DADDY'S HANDS

Words and Music by
HOLLY DUNN

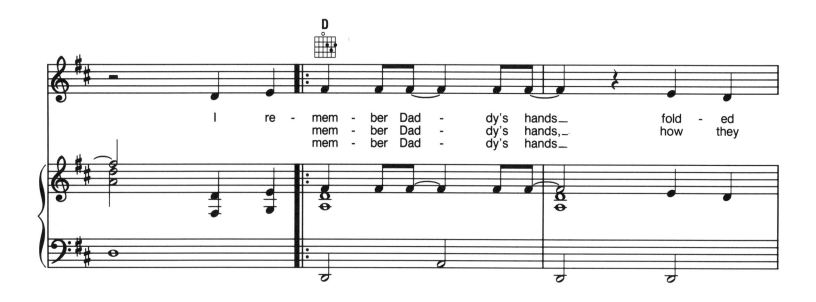

I re - mem - ber Dad - dy's hands___ fold - ed
mem - ber Dad - dy's hands,___ how they
mem - ber Dad - dy's hands___

si - lent - ly in prayer,___ and reach - ing out to hold___
held my Ma - ma tight___ and pat - ted my___ back
work - ing 'til they bled,___ sac - ri - ficed___ un - self -

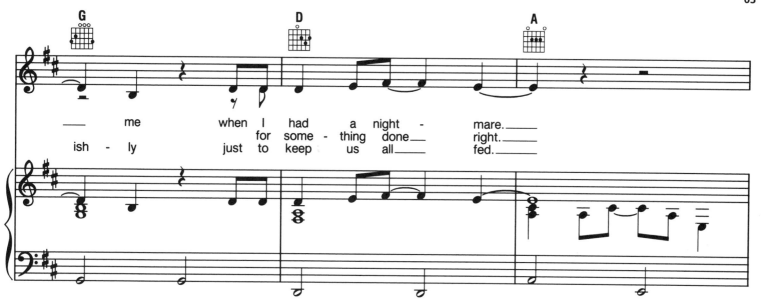

me when I had a night - mare.____

for some - thing done____ right.____

ish - ly just to keep us all____ fed.____

You could read quite a sto - ry____ in the cal -

There are things that I've for - got - ten____ that I

If I could do things o - ver,____ I'd

- lous - es____ and lines.____ Years of work____ and wor -

loved a - bout____ the man,____ but I'll al - ways re - mem -

live my life a - gain____ and nev - er take for grant -

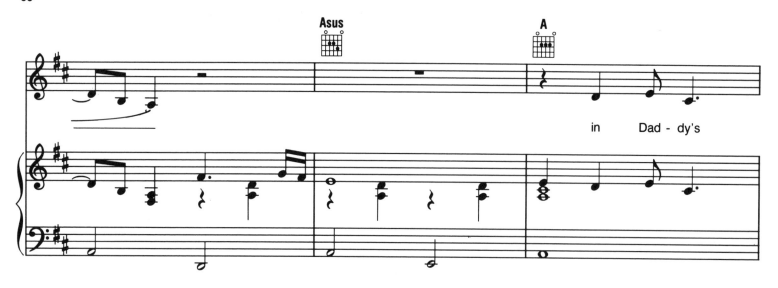

in Dad - dy's

hands.

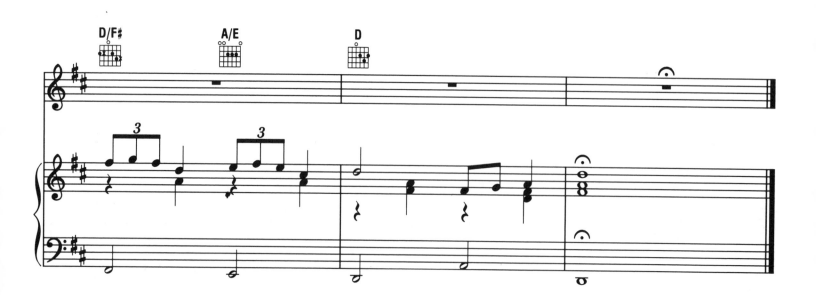

DOWN AT THE TWIST AND SHOUT

Words and Music by
MARY CHAPIN CARPENTER

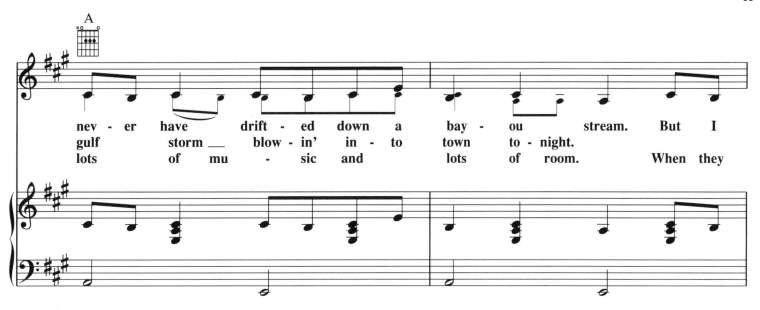

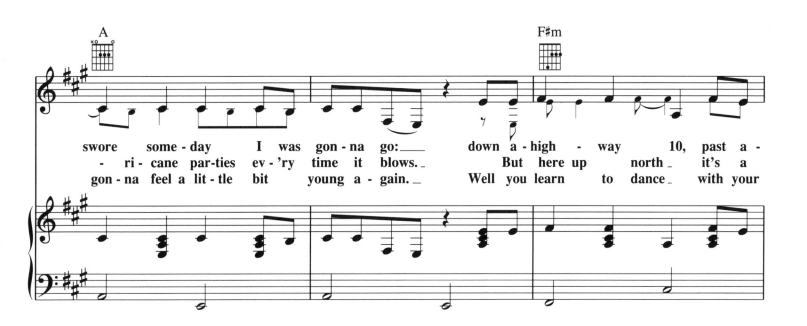

B7
La - fay - ette; there's a Bat - on Rouge. And I
cold, cold rain, and there ain't no cure for my
rock - in' roll, you learn to swing with
E
won't for - get to send you a card with my re - grets 'cause I'm
blues to - day; ex - cept when the pa - per says Beou - so - leil is a
do - si - do. But you learn to love at the fais do do when you
A
nev - er gon - na come back home.
com - in' in - to town. Ba - by, let's go down. It's
hear a lit - tle Jolie Blon.
D
Sat - ur - day night and the moon is out. I wan - na

THE DANCE

Words and Music by
TONY ARATA

but I'd have had to miss the

no chord

dance.

Repeat and Fade

DO YA'

Words and Music by
K.T. OSLIN

Moderately slow, steady beat

Do you still get a thrill__ when you see me com-in' up the hill?__ Hon-ey, now do ya?

Do you whis - per my name__ just to

DON'T CLOSE YOUR EYES

Words and Music by
BOB McDILL

arms___ you still want him I know.
arms___ know-ing he's in your mind.

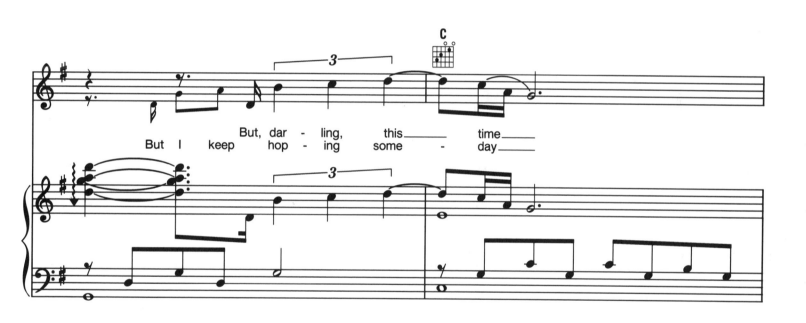

But, dar - ling, this___ time___
But I keep hop - ing some - day___

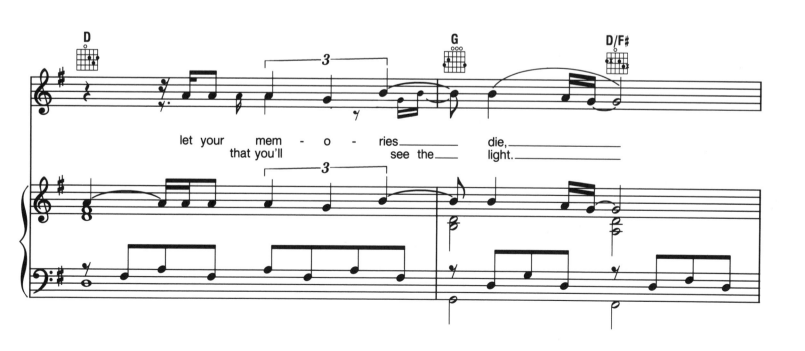

let your mem - o - ries___ die,___
that you'll see the___ light.___

DON'T ROCK THE JUKEBOX

Words and Music by ALAN JACKSON,
ROGER MURRAH and KEITH STEGALL

Additional Lyrics

2. I ain't got nothin' against rock and roll.
But when your heart's been broken, you need a song that's slow.
Ain't nothin' like a steel guitar to drown a memory.
Before you spend your money, babe, play a song for me.
Chorus

EIGHTEEN WHEELS AND A DOZEN ROSES

Words and Music by GENE NELSON
and PAUL NELSON

80'S LADIES

Words and Music by
K.T. OSLIN

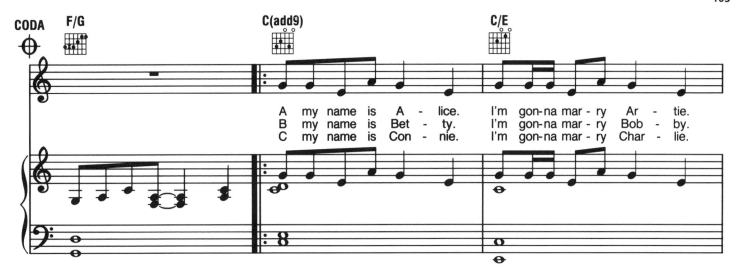

CODA

F/G

C(add9)

C/E

A my name is A - lice. I'm gon-na mar -ry Ar - tie.
B my name is Bet - ty. I'm gon-na mar -ry Bob - by.
C my name is Con - nie. I'm gon-na mar -ry Char - lie.

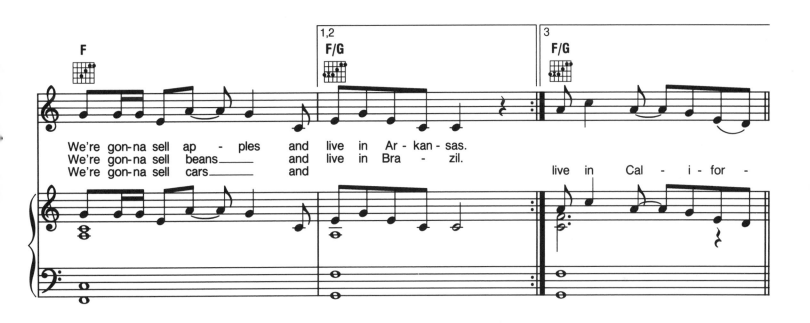

F

1,2
F/G

3
F/G

We're gon-na sell ap - ples and live in Ar - kan - sas.
We're gon-na sell beans_____ and live in Bra - zil.
We're gon-na sell cars_____ and live in Cal - i - for -

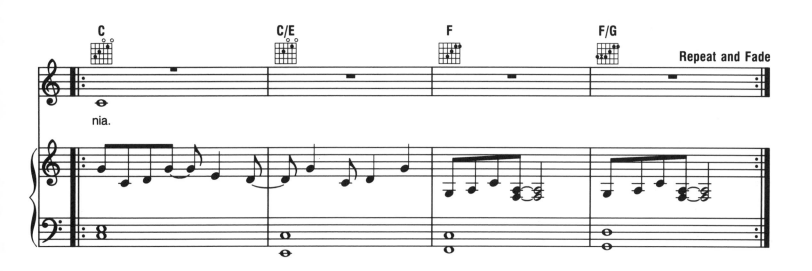

C

C/E

F

F/G

Repeat and Fade

nia.

FOREVER AND EVER, AMEN

Words and Music by DON SCHLITZ
and PAUL OVERSTREET

MCA music publishing

GOD BLESS THE U.S.A.

Words and Music by
LEE GREENWOOD

MCA music publishing

112

FRIENDS IN LOW PLACES

Words and Music by DEWAYNE BLACKWELL
and EARL BUD LEE

Moderately, with a beat

Blame it all on my roots. ___ I
guess I was wrong. ___ I

showed up in boots ___ and ru-ined your black-tie af-fair. ___
just don't be-long, ___ but then ___ I've been there ___ be-fore. ___

The last one to know; ___ the
Ev-'ry-thing's ___ al - right. ___ I'll

118

GONE COUNTRY

Words and Music by
BOB McDILL

She's been play-ing that ___ room ___ on the strip
folk scene's ___ dead, ___ but
mutes to L. A., ___ but

he's hold-ing out ___ in the vil-lage.
for ten years in the Ve-gas.
he's got a house ___ in the Val-ley.

Ev-'ry night she looks ___ in the mir-ror, and she on-ly
He's been writ-ing songs, ___ speak-ing out a-gainst wealth and
But the bills are pil-ing up, and the pop scene just ain't gon-na

GO REST HIGH ON THAT MOUNTAIN

Words and Music by
VINCE GILL

Slowly, in Gospel style

1. I know your
life on — earth was trou-bled — and on - ly you _____ could know — the

2. (See additional lyrics)

pain._____ You weren't a- fraid _____ to face_ the dev - il._____ You're no

stran - ger to ___ the rain. Go rest ___

high on that moun - tain._____ Son, your___

work _____ on _ earth is done. Go to_ heav - en a-shout -

Additional Lyrics

2. Oh, how we cried the day you left us,
   We gathered 'round your grave to grieve.
   I wish I could see the angels' faces
   When they hear your sweet voice sing.
   Chorus

GRANDPA
(Tell Me 'Bout the Good Old Days)

Words and Music by
JAMIE O'HARA

Medium Slow Country

Grand - pa,   tell me 'bout the good old days.___
Grand - pa,   ev - 'ry - thing is chang - in' fast. ___

Some - times ___ it feels ___ like   this world's gone cra- know.
We call ___ it prog - ress,   but I just don't

HE THINKS HE'LL KEEP HER

Words and Music by MARY CHAPIN CARPENTER
and DON SCHLITZ

She makes his cof - fee, she makes _ his _ bed.
She does the car - pool, she P. _ T. _ A.'s.
She packs his suit - case, she sits _ and _ waits

She does the laun - dry, she keeps _ him _ fed.
Doc - tors and den - tists, she drives _ all _ day.
with no ex - pres - sion up - on _ her _ face.

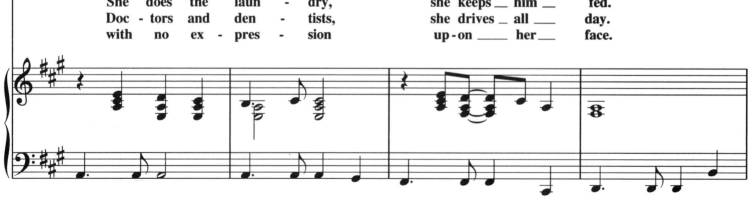

I SWEAR

Words and Music by FRANK MYERS
and GARY BAKER

I see the ques - tions in___ your eyes;___   I know what's weigh -
I'll give you ev - 'ry - thing___ I can;___   I'll build your dreams

HERE'S A QUARTER
(Call Someone Who Cares)

Words and Music by
TRAVIS TRITT

I STILL BELIEVE IN YOU

Words and Music by VINCE GILL
and JOHN BARLOW JARVIS

1. Ev-'ry-bod-y wants__ a lit-tle piece__ of__ my time,__ but still I put__ you at the
2. (See additional lyrics)

end ____ of the line.__ How it breaks__ my heart__ to cause__ you this pain, ____ to see the tears you cry__ fall-in'__ like rain.____ Give me the chance__

Additional Lyrics

2. Somewhere along the way, I guess I just lost track,
Only thinkin' of myself, never lookin' back.
For all the times I've hurt you, I apologize,
I'm sorry it took so long to finally realize.

Give me the chance to prove
That nothing's worth losing you.
Chorus

IF TOMORROW NEVER COMES

Words and Music by KENT BLAZY
and GARTH BROOKS

Some-times late at night, ___
See additional lyrics

I lie a-wake and watch ___ her sleep - ing. ___

She's lost in peace-ful dreams, ___ so I turn

Additional Lyrics

2. 'Cause I've lost loved ones in my life.
Who never knew how much I loved them.
Now I live with the regret
That my true feelings for them never were revealed.
So I made a promise to myself
To say each day how much she means to me
And avoid that circumstance
Where there's no second chance to tell her how I feel. ('Cause)
Chorus

INDEPENDENCE DAY

Words and Music by
GRETCHEN PETERS

THE KEEPER OF THE STARS

Words and Music by DICKEY LEE,
DANNY MAYO and KAREN STALEY

It was ___ no ac - ci - dent, ___
Soft moon - light on your face, ___

me find - ing you.
oh, how ___ you shine.

Some - one ___ had a hand in it ___
It takes ___ my breath a - way ___

A Little Good News

Words and Music by TOMMY ROCCO,
RORY BOURKE and CHARLIE BLACK

LITTLE ROCK

Words and Music by
TOM DOUGLAS

LOOK AT US

Words and Music by VINCE GILL
and MAX D. BARNES

love should be, ___ they'll just ___ look at us.

Chanc - es

LOST IN THE FIFTIES TONIGHT
(In the Still of the Nite)

Words and Music by MIKE REID,
TROY SEALS and FRED PARRIS

1. Close your eyes ba - by,___ fol - low my heart,___
2. *See additional lyrics*

call on the mem - 'ries___ here in the dark.___ We'll let the mag - ic___

take us a - way,___ back to the feel - ing we

Repeat ad lib. and Fade

night.

Shoo - doop, shoo - be doo,

shoo - doop, shoo - be doo, shoo - doop, shoo - be doo, shoo - doop, shoo - be doo.

Additional Lyrics

These precious hours, we know can't survive.
Love's all that matters while the past is alive.
Now and for always, till time disappears,
We'll hold each other whenever we hear:

LOVE, ME

Words and Music by MAX T. BARNES
and SKIP EWING

Moderately slow

1. I read a note __ my grand - ma wrote __ back in __
2., 3. *(See additional lyrics)*

__ nine - teen __ twen - ty three. __

Grand - pa kept __ it in __ his coat __ and he showed it once __ to __ me. __

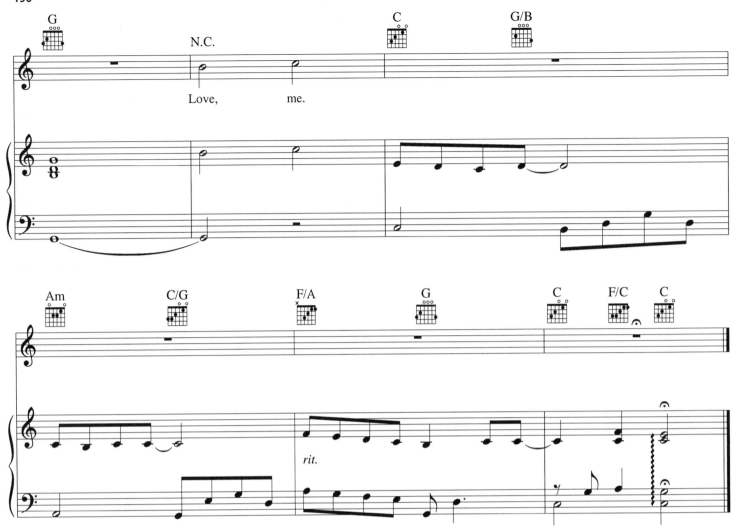

Additional Lyrics

2. We had this crazy plan to meet
   And run away together.
   Get married in the first town we came to
   And live forever.
   But nailed to the tree where we were supposed to meet instead,
   I found this letter and this is what it said,...
   Chorus

3. I read those words just hours before my
   Grandma passed away,
   In the doorway of a church where me and
   Grandpa stopped to pray.
   I know I've never seen him cry in all my fifteen years,
   But as he said these words to her,
   His eyes filled up with tears.
   Chorus

ON THE OTHER HAND

Words and Music by DON SCHLITZ
and PAUL OVERSTREET

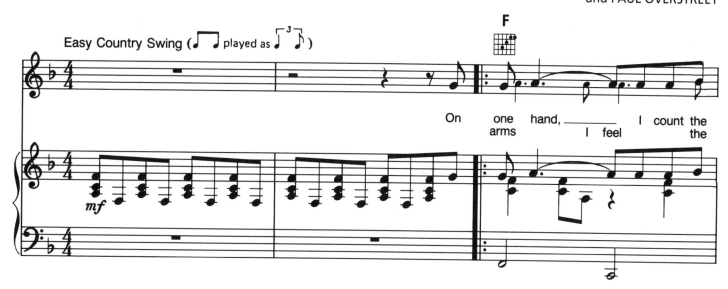

THINKIN' PROBLEM

Words and Music by STUART ZIFF,
DAVID BALL and ALLEN SHAMBLIN

Yes, I ad-mit I got a think-in' prob-lem.

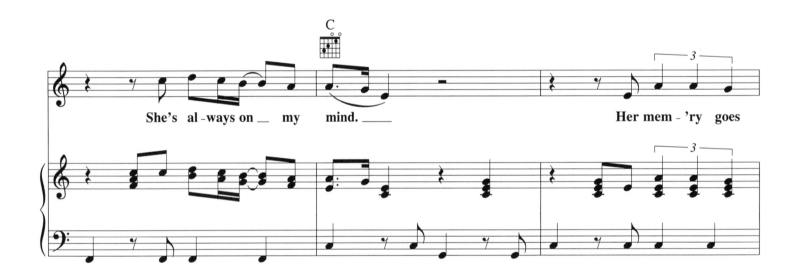

She's al-ways on __ my mind. ____ Her mem-'ry goes

round and round. __ I've tried to quit __ a thou-sand

TIME MARCHES ON

Words and Music by
BOBBY BRADDOCK

WHEN I CALL YOUR NAME

Words and Music by VINCE GILL
and TIM DUBOIS

WHERE'VE YOU BEEN

Words and Music by DON HENRY
and JON VEZNER

THE WIND BENEATH MY WINGS

Words and Music by LARRY HENLEY
and JEFF SILBAR

It must have been cold__ there__ in my shad - ow,

to nev - er have sun - light on your face.

You've been con - tent__ to let me shine,